MY BIG BOOK OF
Christmas
COLORING, SONGS & ACTIVITIES

www.walterfoster.com
6 Orchard Road, Suite 100
Lake Forest, CA 92630

Publisher: Anne Landa
Creative Director: Shelley Baugh
Production Director: Yuhong Guo
Editorial Director: Pauline Molinari
Copy Editors: Janessa Osle, Karen Julian
Production Designer: Debbie Aiken

Printed in China
1 3 5 7 9 10 8 6 4 2

Table of Contents

Christmas Decorating Word Search

Can you find the words listed below?
The words can appear up, down,
forward, backward, and diagonal.

```
W G R C K G F U K K E N X S A P Y H H M G L B
J N V C W M W G E E Q R N D T Q W A C D L G N
L C C W D P S F P H R C H F F O G T H E O C Z
Q G L V J J W N W Q P M P T G O C J T Q M A V
A N H O R N A M E N T B L O W N H Q U H N I
M X J L F H M Z D F I B P S I T G G I G Q D U
W W B Q S X C R P U C S G Z W N G R T N G L K
R O J W Z U F L E T T U T A F N S T B U G E X
E J E U U E X C V N I Z R K E L V E L P P S G
A K Q C G U P M E W U X E I C I H L T R D J A
T Q V U E I Y S J O I D E A G G O K I T O J R
H D X V V F E G M P S R B Q E H L X C G I A L
Z N O A P R H T K P I R H U O T V X A U L A A
V R G H P A I Z U X N A F Q A S X N Q C D C N
X I C R X Y X A N H V E E T K R J U P E C Y D
```

☑ garland   ☑ wreath   ☑ candles

☑ ornament   ☑ poinsettia   ☑ lights

☑ tree   ☑ stocking   ☑ presents

Answer on page 90.

4

Which One Is Different?

One of these groups of ice skaters is different from the rest.
Can you spot the different one?

Answer on page 90.

Message from Santa

Santa left you a message, but it is written in code.
Use the picture clues below to figure out the message.

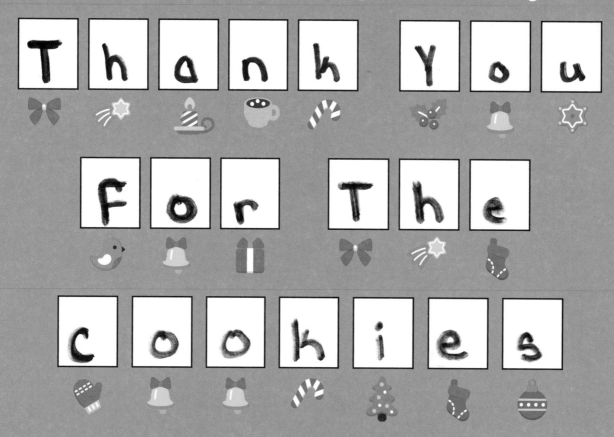

Thank You

For The

cookies

🕯	=A	🌠	=H	🔔	=O	❄	=U
🧤	=C	🎄	=I	🎁	=R	🌿	=Y
🧦	=E	🍬	=K	🔮	=S		
🐦	=F	☕	=N	🎀	=T		

Answer on page 90.

Reindeer Maze

Help this reindeer make his way back to his team!

Answer on page 91.

We Wish You a Merry Christmas

We wish you a Merry Christmas;
We wish you a Merry Christmas;
We wish you a Merry Christmas and a Happy New Year.
Good tidings we bring to you and your kin;
Good tidings for Christmas and a Happy New Year.

Oh, bring us a figgy pudding;
Oh, bring us a figgy pudding;
Oh, bring us a figgy pudding and a cup of good cheer.
We won't go until we get some;
We won't go until we get some;
We won't go until we get some, so bring some out here.

We wish you a Merry Christmas;
We wish you a Merry Christmas;
We wish you a Merry Christmas
and a Happy New Year.

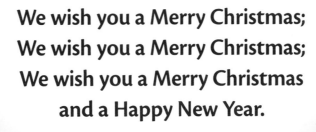

Scrambled Toy List

Can you help Santa figure out this scrambled list of toys?

YICBLEC _Bicycle_

DDYET EBRA _Teddy Bear_

SCPIRESN LODL _Princess Doll_

GOAWN _Wagon_

IAGRUT _Guitar_

EOUTPCRM _Computer_

BODTKAEARS _Skateboard_

ECI TSSAEK _Ice Skates_

Answers on page 91.

Which One Is Different?

One of these Christmas trees is different from the rest.
Can you spot the different one?

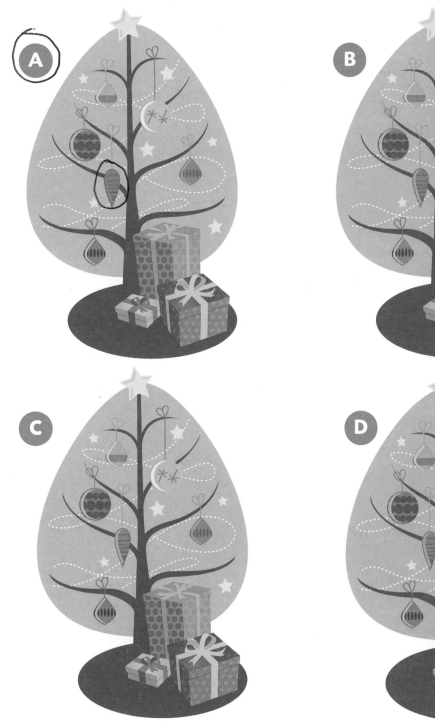

Answer on page 91.

Draw a Gingerbread Man

The gingerbread man is a great holiday treat.
You can make his face, clothes, and buttons with candy
and frosting for extra sweetness!

16

Holiday Sudoku

In each box of nine squares, you can only use the numbers 1 through 9 once! Each row should contain every digit, and each column shoud contain every digit. Give it a try!

9	6	1	3	2	7	5	4	8
7	4	8	1	5	6	9	2	3
5	2	3	9	4	8	6	7	1
3	5	6	4	8	9	7	1	2
8	9	7	6	1	2	3	5	4
4	1	2	7	3	5	8	9	6
2	3	9	8	7	4	1	6	5
6	8	5	2	9	1	4	3	7
1	7	4	5	6	3	2	8	9

Answer on page 91.

Christmas Sweet Treats Word Search

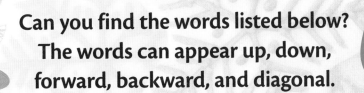

Can you find the words listed below?
The words can appear up, down,
forward, backward, and diagonal.

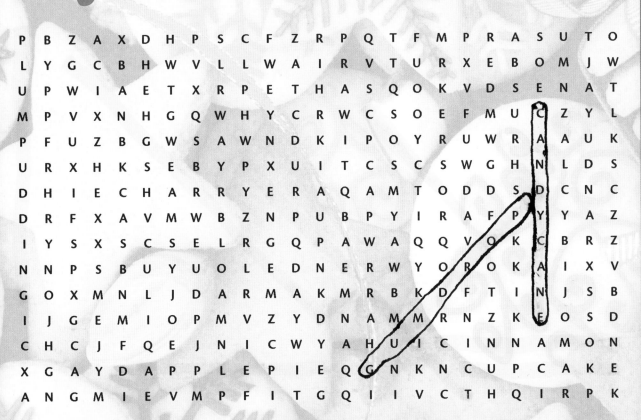

```
P B Z A X D H P S C F Z R P Q T F M P R A S U T O
L Y G C B H W V L L W A I R V T U R X E B O M J W
U P W I A E T X R P E T H A S Q O K V D S E N A T
M P V X N H G Q W H Y C R W C S O E F M U C Z Y L
P F U Z B G W S A W N D K I P O Y R U W R A A U K
U R X H K S E B Y P X U I T C S C S W G H N L D S
D H I E C H A R R Y E R A Q A M T O D D S D C N C
D R F X A V M W B Z N P U B P Y I R A F P Y Y A Z
I Y S X S C S E L R G Q P A W A Q Q V O K C B R Z
N N P S B U Y U O L E D N E R W Y O R O K A I X V
G O X M N L J D A R M A K M R B K D F T I N J S B
I J G E M I O P M V Z Y D N A M M R N Z K E O S D
C H C J F Q E J N I C W Y A H U I C I N N A M O N
X G A Y D A P P L E P I E Q G N K N C U P C A K E
A N G M I E V M P F I T G Q I I V C T H Q I R P K
```

- ☑ candy cane
- ☑ cinnamon
- ☑ cupcake
- ☑ gingerbread
- ☑ peppermint
- ☑ cocoa
- ☑ gumdrop
- ☑ plum pudding
- ☑ apple pie

Answer on page 92.

Polar Bear Maze

Help this polar bear skate back to his family!

START

FINISH

Answer on page 92.

24

Polar Animals Word Search

Can you find the words listed below?
The words can appear up, down,
forward, backward, and diagonal.

```
V P W B X A W J Z I I J T L V N K H H T P
W U L S N O W Y O W L E J D A V S A F R M
A F W A A R M A V V P Z G W W Y Z V N C T
L F F K Z W L A Z N E A C H A R P S E A L
R I O Q H I C A Z I Y I A Z I I H W L I E
U N H L K G O C O Y E K R R Z L P Q C Q G
S L J Z T D T O A R C T I C W O L F W A W
N B K S N V S T L N Y C B G N L N Z J C A
J R C H M L J N S B Z A O E X I R Y T H R
K O B Y K H C R P T E N U S U V N F E K M
O R C R K N Y Q Z J X G T G B W W W N T A
U A P D V M H N U I V R N F Z W W G B A S
S B P O L A R B E A R E I F G K M I R I W
A D G Q V A F H O T P P I J N A R W H A L
R L U U L X B X Y Z T N Q K D T X L I M Q
```

☑ polar bear   ☑ walrus   ☑ arctic wolf
☑ penguin   ☑ narwhal   ☑ harp seal
☑ caribou   ☑ puffin   ☑ snowy owl

Answer on page 92.

Silent Night

Silent night, Holy night
All is calm, all is bright
Round yon virgin, mother and child
Holy infant so tender and mild
Sleep in heavenly peace,
Sleep in heavenly peace.

Silent night, Holy night
Shepherds quake, at the sight
Glories stream from heaven above
Heavenly hosts sing Hallelujah.
Christ our Savior is born,
Christ our Savior is born.

Silent night, Holy night
Son of God, love's pure light
Radiant beams from thy holy face
With the dawn of redeeming grace,
Jesus, Lord at thy birth
Jesus, Lord at thy birth.

On the twelve days of Christmas
my true love gave to me:

12 Drummers Drumming

11 Pipers Piping

10 Lords a Leaping

9 Ladies Dancing

8 Maids a Milking

7 Swans a Swimming

6 Geese
a Laying

5 Golden Rings

4 Calling
Birds

3 French Hens

2 Turtle Doves

and a Partridge in a Pear Tree

Which One Is Different?

One of these nutcrackers is different from the rest.
Can you spot the one that is different?

Answer on page 92.

Color the Santa Scene

Color this Santa scene.
Try and match the image
on the right.

Hark, the Herald Angels Sing!

Hark the herald angels sing
"Glory to the newborn King!
Peace on earth and mercy mild,
God and sinners reconciled."
Joyful, all ye nations rise;
Join the triumph of the skies
With the angelic host proclaim:
"Christ is born in Bethlehem!"
Hark! The herald angels sing
"Glory to the newborn King!"

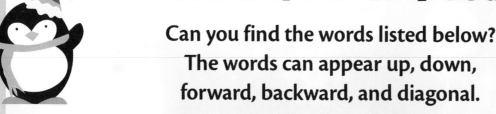

Winter Fun Word Search

Can you find the words listed below?
The words can appear up, down,
forward, backward, and diagonal.

```
L N F K S S N O W B O A R D N W I X W W J O Z
N I N S U Y K S D F O K S P S Q H J L J S H I
F N C V N G S P E K T N N C V V T A H K S X C
K I H I A O B N X E A N O D Y S W C X C V Q Z
O Z Z P C O W Z P B W T W R J O R K P W Q P U
V K F A M L J F Q G V H M R K O G F W E Q O I
Z L N S I B E D L C P T A A A Y R R H M A S Q
K O Q U T B E S W A L O N U U L S O B W I U E
B S E E T H I T Q Y K X Y A O F H S N K D O H
A O P F E S U D A D I E V V F W O T S R S J C
C M O A N M W D Z R Y J J U P L F Y Q G C Q J
B H E T S K A A C V W X M Q S X X O W A A X U
N L I J S Z S N D F Q R T R B L S I H S R E P
P C Y V L L P G C H A A E K N P E C V D F Y I
B Q Y Y Y A U I C E S K A T E S J D R C O U J
```

- [ ] **snowman**
- [ ] **icicle**
- [ ] **snowflake**
- [ ] **sled**

- [ ] **mittens**
- [ ] **skis**
- [ ] **boots**
- [ ] **scarf**

- [ ] **Jack Frost**
- [ ] **ear muffs**
- [ ] **snowboard**
- [ ] **ice skates**

Answer on page 93.

44

Santa's Other Names

Santa goes by many names in the world.
Can you figure out the hidden message to find out Santa's other names?

Italy

France

Russia

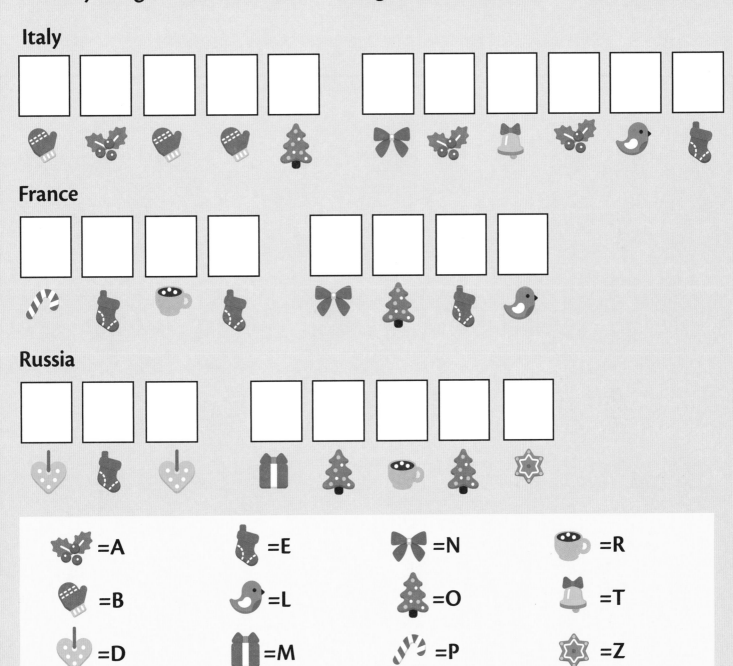

Answers on page 93.

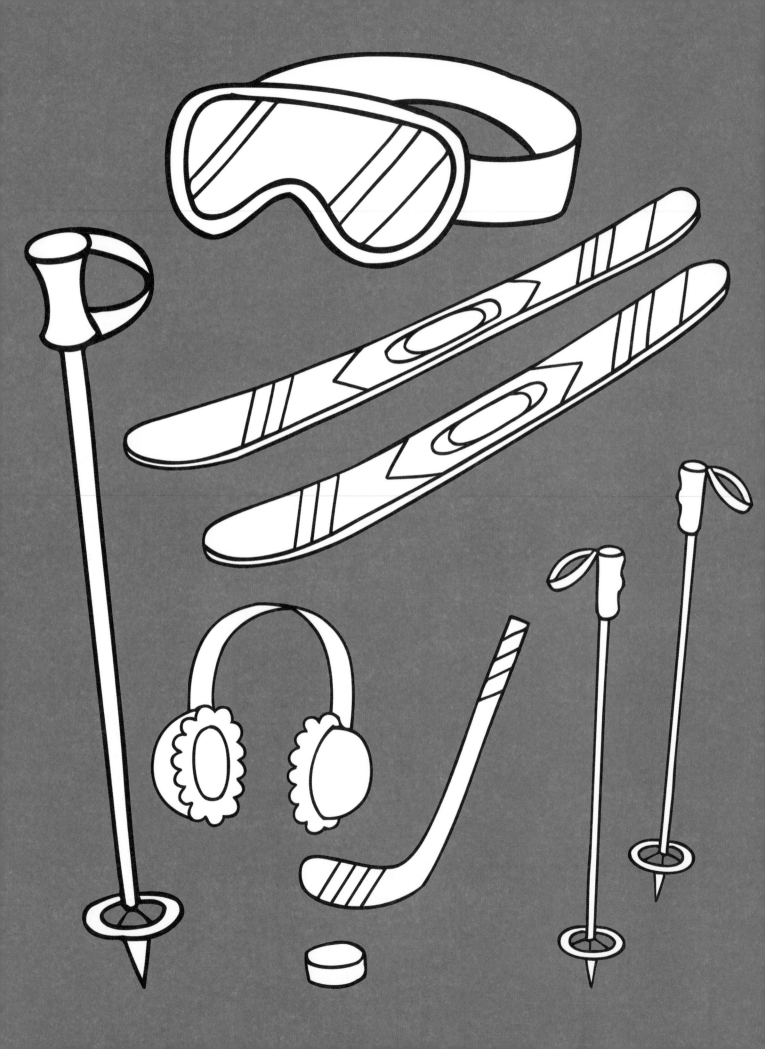

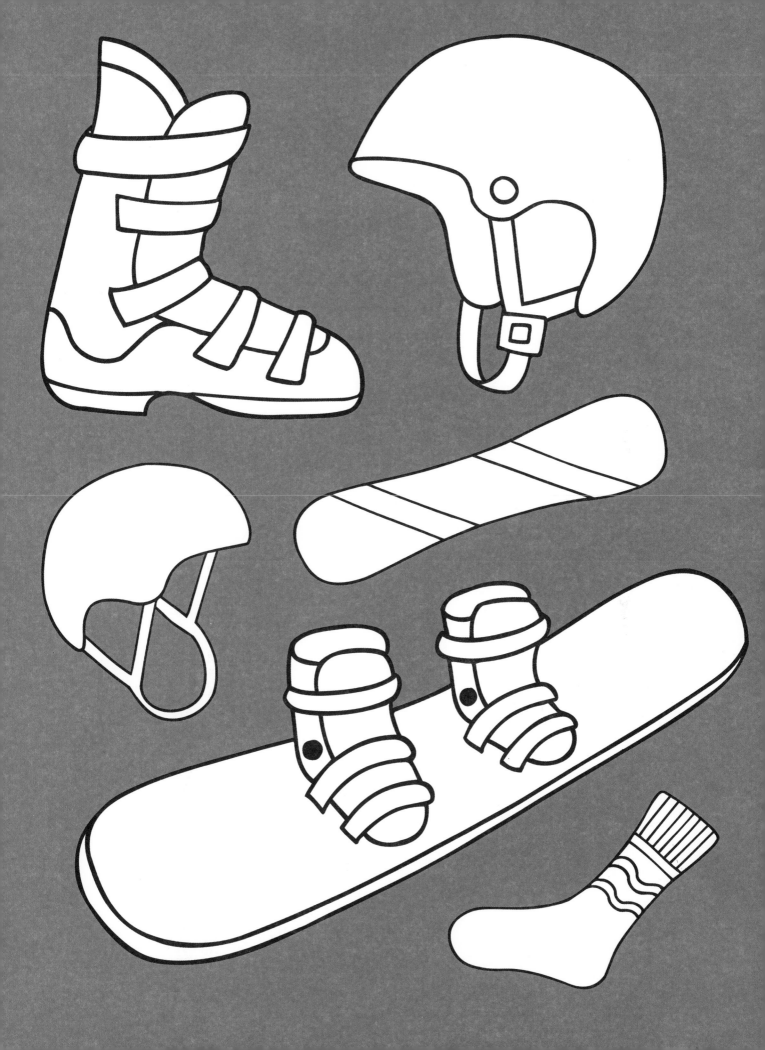

Find the Differences!

Circle 10 differences in this scene.

Answer on page 94.

Penguin Party Maze

Help this little penguin find his way to the party!

START

FINISH

Answer on page 94.

A Visit from St. Nicholas

By Clement Clarke Moore

'Twas the night before Christmas, when all through the house
Not a creature was stirring, not even a mouse;
The stockings were hung by the chimney with care,
In hopes that St. Nicholas soon would be there;
The children were nestled all snug in their beds,
While visions of sugar-plums danced in their heads;
And mamma in her 'kerchief, and I in my cap,
Had just settled our brains for a long winter's nap,
When out on the lawn there arose such a clatter,
I sprang from the bed to see what was the matter.
Away to the window I flew like a flash,
Tore open the shutters and threw up the sash.

The moon on the breast of the new-fallen snow
Gave the lustre of mid-day to objects below,
When, what to my wondering eyes should appear,
But a miniature sleigh, and eight tiny reindeer,
With a little old driver, so lively and quick,
I knew in a moment it must be St. Nick.

More rapid than eagles his coursers they came,
And he whistled, and shouted, and called them by name;
"Now, Dasher! Now, Dancer! Now, Prancer and Vixen!
On, Comet! On, Cupid! On, Donder and Blitzen!
To the top of the porch! To the top of the wall!
Now dash away! Dash away! Dash away all!"

As dry leaves that before the wild hurricane fly,
When they meet with an obstacle, mount to the sky;
So up to the house-top the coursers they flew,
With the sleigh full of toys, and St. Nicholas too.

And then, in a twinkling, I heard on the roof
The prancing and pawing of each little hoof.
As I drew in my head, and was turning around,
Down the chimney St. Nicholas came with a bound.

He was dressed all in fur, from his head to his foot,
And his clothes were all tarnished with ashes and soot;
A bundle of toys he had flung on his back,
And he looked like a pedler just opening his pack.

His eyes—how they twinkled! His dimples how merry!
His cheeks were like roses, his nose like a cherry!
His droll little mouth was drawn up like a bow
And the beard of his chin was as white as the snow;
The stump of a pipe he held tight in his teeth,
And the smoke it encircled his head like a wreath;
He had a broad face and a little round belly,
That shook when he laughed, like a bowlful of jelly.
He was chubby and plump, a right jolly old elf,
And I laughed when I saw him, in spite of myself;
A wink of his eye and a twist of his head,
Soon gave me to know I had nothing to dread;
He spoke not a word, but went straight to his work,
And filled all the stockings; then turned with a jerk,

And laying his finger aside of his nose,
And giving a nod, up the chimney he rose;
He sprang to his sleigh, to his team gave a whistle,
And away they all flew like the down of a thistle,
But I heard him exclaim, ere he drove out of sight,
"Happy Christmas to all, and to all a good night."

Holiday Sudoku

In each box of nine squares, you can only use the numbers 1 through 9 once! Each row should contain every digit, and each column shoud contain every digit. Give it a try!

					3	2	4	8
	1	4		9	6			
	8	3		1				
	6						9	
				5		7	3	
			5	8		4	1	
8	5	6	2					

Answer on page 94.

Joy to the World!

Joy to the world! The Lord is come

Let earth receive her King!

Let every heart prepare His room

And heaven and nature sing

And heaven and nature sing

And heaven, and heaven and nature sing.

Joy to the world! The Savior reigns

Let men their songs employ

While fields and floods

Rocks, hills and plains

Repeat the sounding joy

Repeat the sounding joy

Repeat, repeat the sound joy.

No more let sin and sorrow grow

Nor thorns infest the ground

He comes to make

His blessings flow

Far as the curse is found

Far as the curse is found

Far as, far as the curse is found.

Christmas Crossword

How much do you know about Santa Claus and Christmas?
Solve this puzzle to test your knowledge and bring in the holiday cheer!

ACROSS

4. Reindeer with a shiny nose
5. Jingle ___, jingle ___, jingle all the way!
8. What Santa Claus brings in his sleigh; you'll find it under the tree
10. Santa Claus' employees
12. Where the Clauses live
13. Frozen flakes of it fall from the sky
14. Hung by the chimney with care
15. Christmas is in this season

DOWN

1. A holiday plant. You might get kissed if you stand underneath it!
2. Hang on the tree
3. ___ to the world!
6. Naughty or ___
7. "O Christmas ___, O Christmas ___"
9. St. Nick's favorite snack; milk and ___
11. Frosty the ___

Answers on page 95.

Color the Snowman Scene

Color this snowman scene. Try and match the image on the right.

Santa Claus Word Search

Can you find the words listed below? The words can appear up, down, forward, backward, and diagonal.

- ☐ Santa Claus
- ☐ elves
- ☐ North Pole
- ☐ reindeer
- ☐ sleigh
- ☐ toys
- ☐ chimney
- ☐ presents
- ☐ list
- ☐ Christmas tree
- ☐ stocking
- ☐ cookies

```
C O O K I E S D K Y S O H T Y C S V F C D B S Y Z
X U R K K T E G R U J X Q K O F T L V J O N J P C
R E I N D E E R A D S S T E T Y N G S G N I S D
Y S R X I L L C R P T H O E N S C D L L B C O N
N X E H R H C V E S O M O P C Q I V J E H I Z E N
S X O W D A D N L J M E H C R U T Q S I I F S B S
K C V Z T L T L X S L B M E K E E U N G M D B T V
X D H N M X W W M O P V W B M I S H I H B L T B A
T A A I Z P C R P T R Q R W U R N E G H S F E D T
W S U G M V H H K G D E M A R T F G N K W A P B J
M P I V L N T V G N A L L S D H G D S T J W I U W
N Z Q H N R E P V A S C R V Y V I H P Y S K L A Z
C B L L O E E Y V L H M I V E Y C M G B R U Z V W
O R H N I C Q S G W C C H R I S T M A S T R E E B
```

Answer on page 95.

69

The First Noel

The first Noel the angel did say
Was to certain poor shepherds in fields as they lay:
In fields where they lay keeping their sheep
On a cold winter's night that was so deep.
Noel, Noel, Noel, Noel,
Born is the King of Israel.

They looked up and saw a star
Shining in the east beyond them far:
And to the earth it gave great light
And so it continued both day and night.
Noel, Noel, Noel, Noel,
Born is the King of Israel.

And by the light of that same star
Three wise men came from the country far;
To seek for a King was their intent,
And to follow the star wherever it went.
Noel, Noel, Noel, Noel,
Born is the King of Israel.

This star drew nigh to the north-west;
O'er Bethlehem it took its rest,
And there it did both stop and stay,
Right over the place where Jesus lay.
Noel, Noel, Noel, Noel,
Born is the King of Israel.

Then entered in those wise men three,
Fell reverently upon their knee,
And offered there in his presence
Their gold and myrrh
and frankincense.
Noel, Noel, Noel, Noel,
Born is the King of Israel.

Then let us all with one accord
Sing praises to our heavenly Lord,
That hath made heaven
and earth of nought,
And with his blood mankind has bought.
Noel, Noel, Noel, Noel,
Born is the King of Israel.

Find the Differences!

Circle 10 differences in this scene.

Answer on page 95.

Gingerbread Maze

Help these gingerbread cookies make their way through the maze to their home!

START

FINISH

Answer on page 96.

Gingerbread Cookies

Try making these yummy holiday favorites! Ask a parent for help.

INGREDIENTS

1 cup shortening
1 cup sugar
1 egg
¾ cup molasses
2 tbsp vinegar
5 cups flour

1½ tsp baking soda
½ tsp salt
2-3 tsp ginger
1 tsp cinnamon
1 tsp cloves

INSTRUCTIONS

- Cream together the shortening and sugar.
- Beat in the egg, molasses, and vinegar.
- Sift together the flour, baking soda, salt, ginger, cinnamon, and cloves.
- Blend with the shortening and egg.
- Chill in the fridge for 3 hours.
- Roll dough ½-inch thick and cut with cookie cutter.
- Place on slightly greased cookie sheet, and bake at 375° Fahrenheit for 5 minutes.

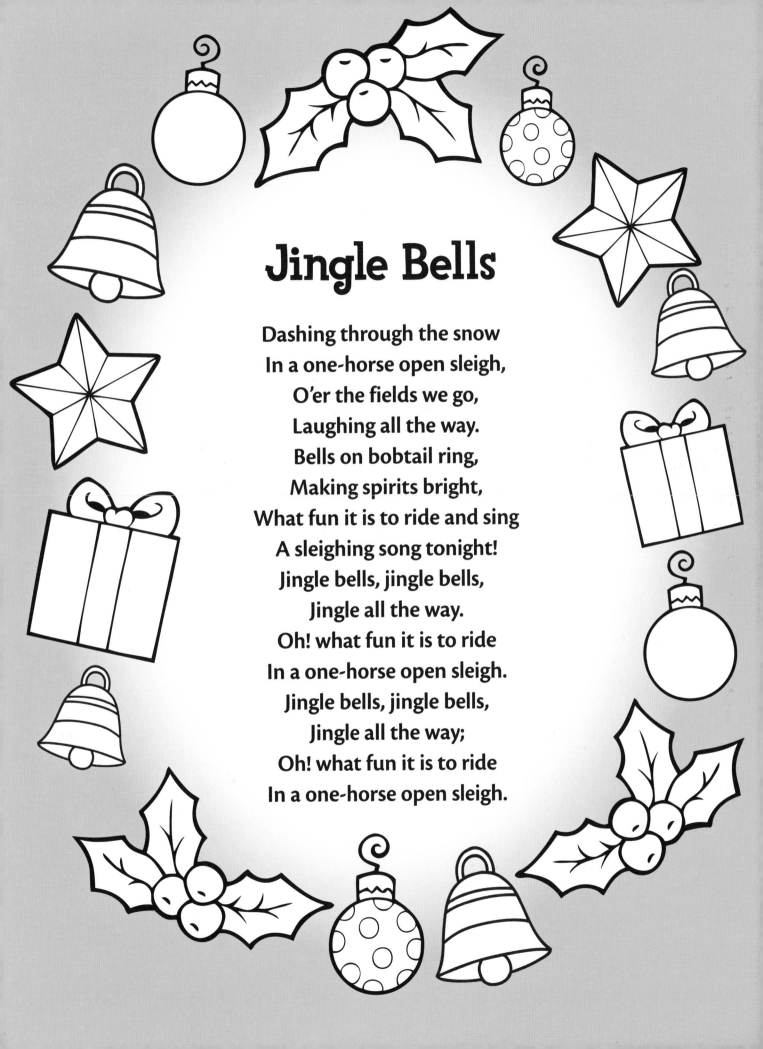

Jingle Bells

Dashing through the snow
In a one-horse open sleigh,
O'er the fields we go,
Laughing all the way.
Bells on bobtail ring,
Making spirits bright,
What fun it is to ride and sing
A sleighing song tonight!
Jingle bells, jingle bells,
Jingle all the way.
Oh! what fun it is to ride
In a one-horse open sleigh.
Jingle bells, jingle bells,
Jingle all the way;
Oh! what fun it is to ride
In a one-horse open sleigh.

Find the Differences!

Circle 10 differences in this scene.

Answer on page 96.

Memory Game

For two or more players

Cut out the cards on the following pages to create a memory game. To play, lay all the pieces facedown. Turn over one piece, and then another. If it is a match, put them to the side. If they don't match, turn them back over and let your opponent try. The one with the most matching pairs wins!

Answer Key

Christmas Decorating Word Search page 4

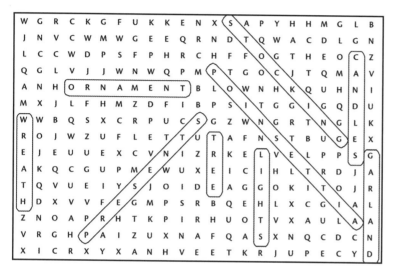

Which One Is Different? page 5

Message From Santa page 8

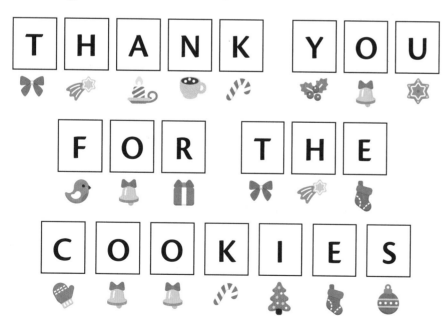

THANK YOU

FOR THE

COOKIES

Reindeer Maze page 9

Scrambled Toy List page 12

BICYCLE

TEDDY BEAR

PRINCESS DOLL

WAGON

GUITAR

COMPUTER

SKATEBOARD

ICE SKATES

Which One Is Different? page 13

A

Holiday Sudoku page 20

9	6	1	3	2	7	5	4	8
7	4	8	1	5	6	9	2	3
5	2	3	9	4	8	6	7	1
3	5	6	4	8	9	7	1	2
8	9	7	6	1	2	3	5	4
4	1	2	7	3	5	8	9	6
2	3	9	8	7	4	1	6	5
6	8	5	2	9	1	4	3	7
1	7	4	5	6	3	2	8	9

Christmas Sweet Treats Word Search page 21

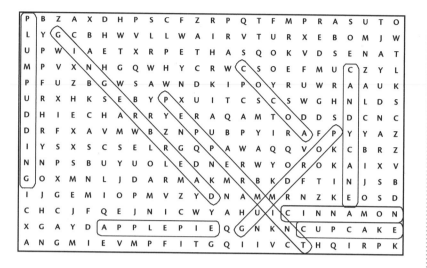

Polar Bear Maze page 24

Polar Animals Word Search page 25

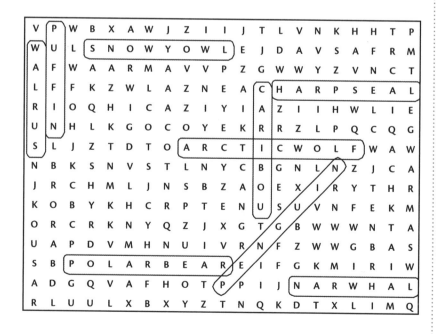

Which One Is Different?
page 38

Winter Fun Word Search page 44

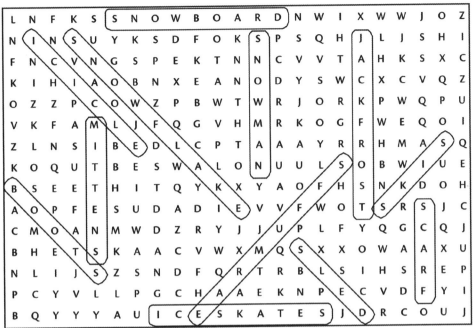

Santa's Other Names page 45

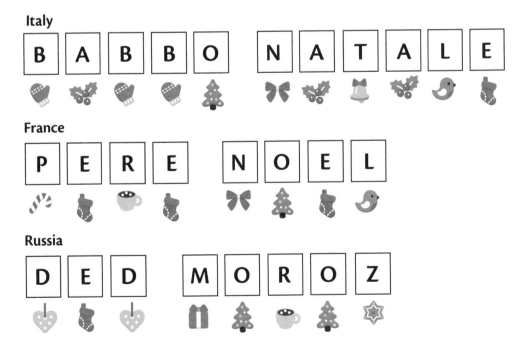

Italy

B A B B O   N A T A L E

France

P E R E   N O E L

Russia

D E D   M O R O Z

Find the Differences! page 50

Penguin Party Maze page 51

Holiday Sudoku page 61

6	9	5	1	7	3	2	4	8
3	7	8	4	2	5	1	6	9
2	1	4	8	9	6	3	5	7
7	8	3	9	1	4	6	2	5
5	6	1	7	3	2	8	9	4
4	2	9	6	5	8	7	3	1
9	3	2	5	8	7	4	1	6
1	4	7	3	6	9	5	8	2
8	5	6	2	4	1	9	7	3

Christmas Crossword page 64

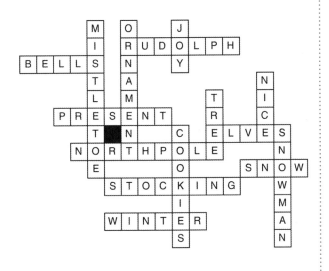

Santa Claus Word Search page 69

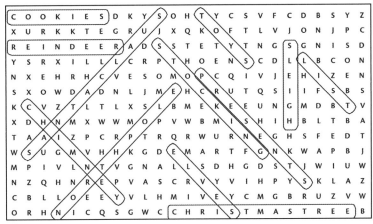

Find the Differences! page 72

Gingerbread Maze page 76

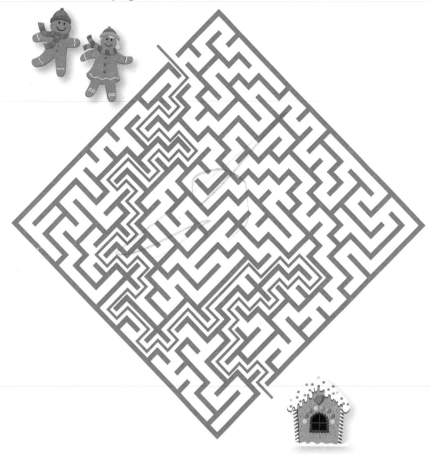

Find the Differences! page 82